Reality Check: Brief Reflections on "Un-conditioning" the Mind

Mitch Halper

Reality Check: Brief Reflections on Un-Conditioning the
Mind
ISBN 978-1-937796-92-1
ALL RIGHTS RESERVED.
Reality Check: Brief Reflections on Un-Conditioning the
Mind Copyright © 2015 Mitch Halper

Edited by Allison Jacobson
Cover art by Louca Matheo
Interior design by Allison Jacobson

Trade paperback Publication May 2015

Kokoro Press is an imprint of Sedonia's Magic Words, Inc.

Published in 2015 by Sedonia's Magic Words, Inc., 10435 Green Trail Dr. N., Boynton Beach, FL 33436.

Manufactured in the U.S.A.

Dedication

This book is dedicated to hippies, those young hairy kids who founded a mass movement against hypocrisy and insanity, who led a revolution against unjust war and nuclear proliferation, who put the F.U. back in fun, who went to the trenches for human rights and animal rights and the rights of the Earth itself, who on so many fronts won so many battles using peace, love, intelligence, music, meditation, art, playfulness and herbs, and never fired a single shot from a single gun.

RIGHT ON!

Foreword

Un-conditioning is about waking up, emerging from a superimposed dream of separate realities into a direct perception of unity, which is life as it is. It is what's commonly called "spiritual work."

All of the great traditions offer teachings and methodologies to enable this process of awakening. Unfortunately, the conditioned mind can easily turn anything into a conditioned response. When that happens, the conditioned view that was supposed to be eradicated is actually strengthened, and the mind becomes even more narrow and closed. We are all too painfully aware of the rampant rise of fundamentalism, intolerance and violence stemming from so-called religious values.

The brief reflections in this book can, I hope, illuminate the pitfalls of traditional spiritual work and broaden the possibilities of the path to awakening, which is simply, our birthright.

Introduction

I hope this little book needs no introduction. If it does, write to me and let me know, and I'll write an introduction. Thank you. Mitch

Okay. Some people read it and asked for an introduction.

On November 1, 1976, the day before Jimmy Carter was elected president, I was given the greatest gift of my life in the form of a spiritual awakening I remembered my own true self. The grace clarity and joy lasted for four glorious days and three wonderful nights and completely changed my life both in its direction and its quality. Nothing would ever be the same. I need to state that prior to my awakening I had never been involved in any formal spiritual training and only sought such training afterwards.

In 1992, shortly after moving to Florida, a bunch of people—and I do mean a bunch—of "poor misguided souls", asked if we could form a group with me as its guide. Oy vey! I was really reluctant, as I had been in groups and schools and zendos and ashrams, and even though they all had something good to say, they also had something that struck me as destructive to the actual work they espoused: Too much Dogma. They were loaded with -isms. These -isms invariably led to conformity, and conformity is the death of innocence. I certainly didn't want that for my new friends. Also, I had read a quote from Ramana Maharshi in which he says quite plainly, "Being a spiritual teacher is an onerous job." So of course I said okay.

It all started well enough with our little group, but after a short time, I realized how inadequate I was and am to really help anyone in the way my heart would wish. That's when I discovered the deep significance of Dialogue and the Way of Surrender and that was my second great awakening.

Enclosed in this little pamphlet are just a few thoughts that I felt might be of some help, said in a way that I hope is more reachy than preachy, although a little preachy, and also a little funny. I hope these brief insights offer a compassionate, unconventional perspective, and that you, dear reader, may find them comforting, stimulating, and perhaps a bit enlightening.

Our group is still meeting after twenty-three years three times a week, and to my surprise and delight, new knowledge is always rising and love and respect always growing.   MH 2014

some people

It has come to my attention on many occasions, that the voice inside of me that tells me to do a certain thing, is the exact same voice that later on criticizes me for having done exactly what it told me to do in the first place. There is just no pleasing some people.

reality check

Enlightenment, which is Reality, is self-love and manifests as compassionate non-attachment or liberation through understanding. When you see or understand that you are really good, already really good it brings happiness and a feeling of being completely connected to life., All the strategies to be good and the masks that have been created are seen as superfluous and simply fall away. This removal of the "veils" allows the direct and unclouded perception of what has always been there.

You don't need to become a good or lovable person. You don't need to make some herculean effort to become safe or happy or to acquire knowledge or to gain approval. That's why *real life* is joyous, because it is effortless.

So much of what is called spiritual work is people trying to be good, to get it right, to succeed, so that the guru or god or mommy or daddy will love them. It is like some weirdly choreographed courtship.

In the first spiritual group I attended, the men were *required* to wear jackets and ties and the ladies had to wear long skirts no matter what the weather was like. Homosexuality was considered unacceptable. One had to sit in rock hard chairs, perfectly upright, for hours on end and listen to lectures and learn Sanskrit and calligraphy and sewing and had to maintain all the school buildings in immaculate condition as an unpaid service. One had to eat silently, work silently. All these things were required not elective. Oh well, you get the picture. *All this to find what we already have.* We need to stop denying how dissatisfying, dehumanizing and shitty this kind of coercion is. There is no heart in it at all.

In reality, the person struggling to connect with reality, struggling to find love, is already completely loved and connected but doesn't recognize it. The old analogy is of a man standing in water up to his neck and complaining that he's dying of thirst. This is quite literally true.

For many years I've been telling people that spiritual work is stopping or more specifically, surrendering. Meditation is non-doing. Surrender is non-doing. Love is non-doing. If you have to do something to get enlightened, then what you're looking for isn't freedom or love, for it is just another conditional relationship with life.

Whatever obstacles you may have to loving yourself as you are right now, I can promise you, they are all unreal. You learned them somewhere from someone who didn't care and didn't know you.

It doesn't matter how awful or ugly your secret is, your past actions, your dreadful mistakes, lies or transgressions. One thing is certain, not loving yourself right now isn't helping anyone, isn't fixing anything or undoing any harm that may have been done. Seeing the misunderstanding that has been guiding the efforts to acquire love or peace will make you appreciate the uselessness of them.

The most unselfish thing is not to embark on some heroic spiritual journey but to drop or surrender any obstacles, any conditions to love immediately so you can finally make a proper amends. Do you see?

Spirituality is the unclenching of a fist, the unfolding of a heart, the non-becoming, non-forcing, non-attached compassion, which is, and has always been, the Real.

escaping reality

For years I've heard the expression 'escaping from reality' but I'm absolutely convinced that no one is trying to escape from reality. It's not reality that creates the fear and longing and brokenness in our lives from which we would wish to escape. Reality is satisfying, not frightening, not empty. It is an illusion of reality created by ignorance that is so unbearable. The illusion of separateness, the illusion of connectedness to disconnected hardened hearts and closed minds is the source of the suffering that we would all wish to be free of.

identification or perpetuating fear

The ego is a multi-faceted mask we create and wear so as not to affront the ignorance of those around us and in this way, to protect ourselves from their wrath.

Unfortunately, the only way to be sure that we continue to feel safe is to forget why we created the mask in the first place, so as never to revisit that awful, frightening time. In this way we come to believe that the mask is real, which is why the ego is so convoluted.

In forgetting ourselves and forgetting how we have forgotten, we become the people we ourselves feared. So now, instead of finding safety, we are continuously threatened. We carry the environment with us that we originally sought to escape.

restored

In creating a separate self to deal with overwhelming grief, we are like a fallen angel. When we stop creating a separate self and feel our grief, we are as one restored. "The kingdom of Heaven is within you."

The whole creation belongs to those who have stopped making separateness.

stucked

Fear and anger are the two sides of one coin. I'm afraid of anger and angry over being afraid.

But what is this coin made of? It's made of a dog chasing its own tail or barking at its own reflection.

In order to find our humanity, we really must stop living like animals.

addiction

If people knew how to love, they would not become addicted. Instead of seeking solace in alcohol, drugs, gambling, shopping, or promiscuous sex, they would simply comfort themselves by resting in their own hearts. The reason addiction is often inherited is because the children of addicts grow up in the same loveless environment that the addicted parent lives in. After all children live in their parents' heart.

If only the addict would admit that they did not know how to love, everything could change. The First Step in the 12-Step program reads: *We admit we are powerless over our addiction and our lives have become unmanageable.* I think it would be more accurate if it were to say, *We admit we do not know how to love but humbly wish to learn.* In Program, there is a saying that "we are only as sick as our secrets." Not knowing how to love is the darkest secret of all.

don't kill the ego

In so much of spiritual literature, there is a belief that the ego must die, but I have not found this to be true and it doesn't stand to reason that in the discovery of love and Truth, violence to anything would be the outcome. Quite to the contrary, ego must be understood, and how can we possibly understand something when we are trying to kill it?

The key to the inner work, in my experience, is for ego to become transparent, not dead. *Ego is a self that was given to us by others. It is not our own.* When we know that, the mind is filled with light This light, the light of Wisdom, of understanding, acts as an X-ray to the density of ego, hence, transparency. Once you can see through ego, it is no longer a problem, as it is no longer an obstacle to understanding. In fact, understanding the ego has been the path to Wisdom.

One of the unexpected benefits of a mind that is filled with light is how quiet it is. Light, after all, makes no sound. Struggling with the ego is noisy, as struggle is noisy, and the mechanical mind created by blind obedience to others, is also noisy because machinery makes a lot of noise.

sufficient

When I woke up all those years ago I was flooded with understanding and love. In fact, where love and knowledge meet, I came to understand, is what is called wisdom.

When you truly love something, you join with it, and so you fully understand it, and when you really understand something, you can't help but love it, as you see its heart.

One of the most important things I learned when I woke up was that the *Truth is always sufficient*, that no matter how things appear to the mind, the Truth is the only satisfying, complete, right thing and the truth is I am complete within myself without effort or constraint, and so are we all.

being

To become enlightened is impossible. To be enlightened is natural. Becoming is a struggle. Being is surrender of struggle.

It is essential to keep the goal in mind, but to keep the goal in mind is not struggle toward the goal. It is the remembrance that the freedom from struggle is the goal.

I-I, captain Ramana

There was a man named Ramana Maharshi who had a big spiritual awakening. He also had about the sweetest most peaceful face that you could ever hope to see. If you are not familiar with him or have never seen his picture, you're really missing something. He woke up when he was sixteen and never went back to sleep, which must have been the reason he had such a nice face. He used to say that when you wake up, you find the "I-I". I believe what he meant by this was that when you wake up, you wake up by loving the personal self and in loving the personal self, you find the universal Self, that these two I's can now live together in a connected and harmonious way. That strikes me as the perfect description of peace.

dialogue

I have found that dialogue is a most direct and vital path to enlightenment, or the discovery of Truth. This is not a new or original insight. I'm in the excellent company of Socrates, the Buddha, Krishnamurti, and the long, noble history of the Talmud and The Upanishads.

Dialogue includes within it, the great paths of: Inquiry—as the questions naturally arise as to, "Who am I? What is this world? And Why am I here?" Meditation—in the form of sensitive, attentive listening, clarity of mind and precision of speech. Humility—in the surrendering of pre-conceptions to serve as a vessel of possibilities. Devotion—in the bond of friendship and mutual care that is the basis of trusting communication, and of course, Awakening itself, in that the walls of ego-centricity must turn into doors and windows in order to see clearly what points of view have the most merit and the discipline to hammer and test these views and sound them for the ring of Truth.

Hence, dialogue is a complete path: Surrender, friendship, service, inquiry, discrimination, humility, meditation, communion, and perhaps most importantly of all, the humanity intrinsic in the process itself.

"un-conditioning"

The Truth is subversive, revolutionary. That's why it has always been suppressed. The truth is that no one *really* wants the latest cell phone or computer or car or a lover or a child, or to be an American or a Buddhist or a lawyer or any of the *seemingly* desirable things people pursue. The Truth is, everyone just wants to be happy. Somewhere along the line, we've been conditioned to believe that happiness depends on getting, having and becoming, that happiness is conditional. But of course it is not. If it were, then happiness would be dependency, and we all know that dependency is actually misery.

Again and again, we see people and know people with all these conditions met: right car, gorgeous spouse, cute kids, terrific religion, plenty of money, great job, etc. and they still aren't happy. In fact, many of them are actually depressed or addicted or even suicidal. Yet we don't seem to realize what we're seeing. What we're seeing is that happiness is *always* unconditional. How subversive is that? Happiness *never* depends on something. In fact, it depends on nothing, literally. Picture a place where no conditions for happiness exist, no coercion, no politics, no religious prejudice, no possessiveness or nationalism or competition, or fear. Where all of that stuff is gone, happiness is naturally there. As that good soul John Lennon sang, "Imagine there's no heaven." Heavenly, isn't it?

holy children

It is a terrible disservice to Truth to think of men like Socrates, Jesus, the Buddha, Lao Tzu, Moses or Mohammed, as gods or prophets, or even as holy men. In fact, they were simply Real, just true to themselves, true to life. When we elevate them we reduce ourselves and we reduce our possibilities as fellow children of the same father and sadly, absolve ourselves of the awe-inspiring responsibility we were born to, which is *to be true to our nature.*

It is true that their words and their lives offer us a depth of wisdom that is not often seen or heard but the real Book of Life is written in every heart. In the opening of our heart, we can read the wordless poetry of the startling revelations and spontaneous joys that we see in the glow of wonder shining in the eyes of children. We are, all of us, those children.

measure

No sane person would force their foot into a shoe that was the wrong size. You would end up in terrible pain, and possibly disabled. We should never try to fit our foot to the shoe. Yet how many of us have adapted ourselves to a way of life that just doesn't fit right? A life is a lot more than a foot. Lao Tzu said, "The journey of a thousand miles begins with a single step." I hope your shoes fit right if you're going to make that journey.

the law

Birth, race, nationality, gender, creed, and social station and all that comes with the 'where' and the 'when' of life are circumstantial. We should never convict anyone, including ourselves, on circumstantial evidence.

the THInner Circle

The only reason the wisdom club seems so small or exclusive is because very few people want to join. If someone doesn't treasure something, why should they pursue it or find it? Most of us, it seems, want to join the money club or the family club, or the country club, or Sam's Club, and so these clubs have millions and millions of members, while very few are interested in the wisdom club.

It is one aspect of justice that each should get what they truly treasure. It takes an awful lot of energy to build and run a business or to go to law school or medical school or to raise a family. It takes a similar degree of commitment to find Wisdom, but honestly, I don't think that's the problem.

I blame the bad press and the bad stuff that surrounds Truth-seeking for people's aversion to Wisdom and the subsequent attraction to the Disney life. It's partly a matter of advertising or marketing. There is not one passage in the New Testament that I'm aware of where Jesus is having a really good day. In the entire Pali canon attributed to the Buddha, as far as I know, no one seems to be interested at all in having fun.

I'm being slightly facetious, but the problem is really quite complicated. It's partly the leaders who never wanted to lead, the followers who were too often either credulous or unscrupulous, the teachings which have been tampered with and often misinterpreted, and of course, the terrible fate of many of the good people who were simply seeking the Truth and wishing humanity well, for instance, Socrates, poisoned, Jesus, crucified, Jeremiah, stoned to death, Joan of Arc, burned at the stake, and more recently, Gandhi, shot, Martin Luther King, Jr., shot, John Lennon, shot, and the Dalai Lama, exiled.

So if the world's history by and large, paints such a bleak picture of the life of wise people, it's no wonder that no one is breaking down the door to club Wisdom or that the Wisdom writings seem esoteric, or that the Inner Circle cookouts are so sparsely attended.

lighten up

For too many years, I attended a "spiritual" school, and with very few exceptions, the students were like robots, stiff, largely uncompassionate, elitist, and very, very serious. At one point, we found out that the head of this school was a closeted alcoholic. Frankly, I wasn't surprised, though I found it sadly ironic that the leader of a spiritual school had helped to create an environment in which she didn't feel safe enough to tell the truth. It all fit.

In Zen and in certain yogic meditation, people are instructed to sit in a rigid posture for twelve or more hours a day for a week at a time with only short breaks to stretch their legs and to have brief, silent meals. Then of course, there is the life of celibacy which has been imposed and accepted in various priesthoods, nunneries and monasteries, and is often considered a necessary condition for holiness.

Enlightenment is to lighten up. I have nothing but admiration for any valid path, but how compassion can arise from coercion defies reason. How finding what is natural and flowing can come from an unnatural and stilted process is quite beyond understanding. If Life really wanted all of that seriousness, It would not have given us flexible spines, a sense of humor and mischief, or sensitive and weird-looking genitals. It seems to me a subtle form of arrogance to deny these happy gifts.

This view will probably not be a popular one with the spiritual crowd.

not the Ten Commandments, not the eightfold path, but the nine things which means between 8 and 10

1: Rigidity is not attentiveness.

2: Seriousness is not sincerity.

3: Conformity is not humility, respect, or surrender.

4: Fear of God is not love of anything.

5: Self-denial is not sacrifice, which actually means to make sacred.

6: Pushing gives hemorrhoids, not enlightenment.

7. Enlightenment is not solitary or isolated. It's unity.

8: Dialogue is a direct path because it puts communion at its center. Dialogue is not following or believing or reading or ritual. It is communicating. Dialogue is not $150.00 for a 50 minute hour or a thousand dollars for a weekend seminar. It is not a religion or a philosophy. It is friendship.

9: Wisdom is never a commodity. It is a gift.

hungry

Greed, hatred, fear, pride, and the whole host of misery-producing thoughts, feelings and actions, only exist in the absence of the Real.

In the same way an imaginary meal would not satisfy our hunger nor an imaginary bath cleanse our bodies, so too the imaginary lives we lead are dissatisfying and leave us hungry and dirty. This illusion of life is based on an imagined self, someone limited, separate and special, identified with arbitrary characteristics such as race, religion, nationality, gender, physique, wealth or poverty. None of this is the real person, and to believe that it is, leaves us desperate and craving something substantial. Frightened by our own ignorance and feeling lost and alone, we unwittingly redouble our grip on what we have already mistakenly claimed as real.

sadness

When anything hurts our heart, love takes the form of sadness.

invalid

All of us struggle with concerns of internal versus external validation. But what if the question itself or the struggle itself is wrongheaded? Why do we require validation of any sort to begin with? On some level we must believe ourselves to be fundamentally invalid. Basically unacceptable.

If in fact, we are fundamentally flawed, then no amount of work can possibly straighten us out, and if we are not "factory defects" then what's this business about validation?

I think people seek validation instead of seeking satisfaction, and I believe this is a form of punishment.

Little children are deeply aware of their parents' inadequacies, and as such, are guilty of clarity, which is a betrayal of the false. Being ashamed of our parents' nakedness is the root of seeking validation.

not this

The Real cannot be named or known as an object of observation. Anything that can be named or known as an object cannot be real. That does not mean that it doesn't exist, just that it doesn't exist as a name or form in Reality. What it really is, is something altogether different, something so refined that it cannot be defined. Something wondrous.

exorcism

It's a terrible thing when most of humanity doesn't value what's real and lives lost in illusion and in denial of their loss. For anyone wishing to find what's real, they are confronted on every side by perverted views and unnatural activities all hiding under the guise of convention and normalcy. Nothing less "dramatic" than an exorcism is necessary to rid oneself of the demons of conventionality and the popular mythology which is a wretched complicity of sleep.

This exorcism requires no priest, no intercessor of any kind, only an open, questioning mind. That openness is in and of itself, the act of purification.

temptation

"Lead us not into temptation, but deliver us from evil." Why would anyone be tempted to do evil? Evil is 'live' spelled backwards (which is rather witty). So why would anyone want to live backwards? It's as though they were retreating from life rather than advancing into it. Only fear of life would cause such retreat. Fear of facing life would create a backwards mind, a backwards heart and a view that could be called evil. And why would anyone not want to turn toward what is Real? Only through misunderstanding, misconstruing what is unreal for what is real or a lie for what is true. This misunderstanding would drain our faith in the goodness of life. *The basic assumption of evil intent and temptation as something to resist is, itself, highly questionable.*

I would pray, please, lead me into temptation because it is the good things that tempt me. My heart knows innately what is good, the things that are real and sweet and fine. It's a startling fact that in nature sweet-tasting foods are never poisonous.

sex

People who are sexually active have found enlightenment and people who are not sexually active have found enlightenment. How can an unconditional state be based on any set of conditions? Does Grace suddenly withdraw in the presence of nudity or squishy noises? Does unconditional Love say 'no' to men who desire men, but 'yes' to men who desire women?

It is superimposed limitation that denies the ever present Grace, not sex.

A home made Prayer

On this day I pray, may I surrender my mind to Truth, my heart to Love, and my actions to Harmlessness.

Amen.

Om Tat Sat.

choked up

I've come to see that when I'm choked with emotion, it is because I learned somewhere that I'm not allowed to know or feel or say what is really going on inside me. My feeling gets stuck between my heart and mind or my knowledge gets stuck between my mind and heart. In either case I'm not free to express what I feel and know. Hopelessness and ignorance are the direct fruit of this prohibition. After all what is the point in knowing and feeling if I can't share, can't communicate? What is the point of having something wise to say if my voice goes unheard?

In *The Upanishads* there is a beautiful prayer: "They have put a golden stopper into the neck of the bottle. Pull it, Lord! Let out Reality! I am full of longing."

possession

The word 'covenant' is usually translated as 'contract.' But in fact, it is from the Hebrew, *kavannah* which means 'intention.'

Intention is nine-tenths of the law, not possession. If someone accidentally runs over your foot, it may hurt just as much physically as if someone runs over it on purpose, but the psychological and emotion impact is completely different. Our manmade laws recognize this distinction.

In reality, there is no possession, as the Universe owns everything. It giveth and It taketh away. There is no 'my family' as everyone is made from the same fire, blood, air and mud. No 'my country' or 'my religion' as all receive from the same Earth and are in the same boat and although there are never any survivors everything is continuously recycled and made new. We live under the same universal laws and lawgiver and under the same stars and sky. We are quite literally together forever.

spend on love, not fear

If we ever want world peace we must treat our enemies as we, ourselves, wish to be treated. Instead of spending trillions on bombs and guns and armies, we should help our enemies build hospitals, roads, schools and farms. We want safety, security, health and happiness, and so do they. We spend a pittance on our Peace Corps yet trillions on our War corps. How, exactly, does that reflect the highest Christian value: to "love your enemy?"

If we just took all the money spent in this country in one year at gun shows and bought toys and medicine for the poor children of the world, I am confident we would see peace in our time. How can anyone continue to hate those who love the little children? Could *you* possibly wish to terrorize someone who has just saved *your* child's life?

freedom

Heaven is here. Hell is here. Heaven is reality. Hell is not knowing what is real. Another way to say this is that Heaven is unity and Hell is not knowing that unity. Another way to say this is, "Hear, O Israel, the Lord our God, the Lord is One." Or "No man can serve two masters," or, "The Truth shall make us free." Which implies that the untruth shall enslave us.

sin?

If a child is scorched and burned by overexposure to the sun, should we blame the sun? Or should we say someone ignored and neglected the child?

Now if that burned, neglected child should live for years in a cave in darkness out of fear of the sun's heat, it might prove difficult to convince him or her to come out. We may say again and again, "It was not the fault of the sun that you were burned but of ignorance and neglect." And if the child should never come out, what a heartache that would be, but who could blame him?

re-enactment

I've noticed, and maybe you have too, that many of us tend to get in the same sort of relationships again and again. In other words, we gravitate toward the same people and make the same mistakes in relationship that lead to all sorts of suffering, broken-heartedness and disappointment. We've all heard other people say, and have probably said ourselves, "What is wrong with me why do I keep picking these losers?"

I think the reason for this is that there is unfinished business from one or more very early, painful relationships that we didn't learn the lessons that the relationships were meant to teach us.

You see, I don't think it's the person whom we choose that is the problem. I think the problem is that *we believe whoever hurt us when we were young is the only person who can possibly heal us* and so we are drawn again and again to the same type of person who hurt us hoping that this time we can get healed. Again, *Since they hurt us, only they can heal us.*

This is a terrible mistake. We mistake the *carrier of a disease for the disease itself. We mistake the carrier for the cause.* The disease itself is always some form of ignorance not a particular person. Whether it was neglect, abuse, carelessness, or abandonment, it all stemmed from the act of ignoring the truth of the child — the precious innocence, the vulnerability, the need for freedom to explore under a benevolent umbrella of watchful kindness, the little moment to moment awareness that prevents harm.

The only cure for this disease of ignorance is care, what Buddhists call mindfulness. or presence of mind and heart. Presence is a word so rich in meaning: to be in this moment, to offer for acceptance, to make a gift of, to view or notice, to show up fully, completely. It is this gift of presence that was so sorely lacking and the resultant craving for this gift that drives us.

We already know picking "losers" time and again doesn't work, as anyone who carries this disease can only re-infect us, never cure us. In point of fact the continuous re-infection through seeking the wrong person-thing again and again is the way the disease replicates itself. We are treating the hurt child the exact way she was treated in the original unhealthy relationship, ignoring the real need and unquestioningly following a harmful impulse, reenacting something we never wanted or needed in the first place.

pain

Pain is our friend, our guide. If you get a pain in your foot, you don't look up at the sky, you look at your foot, of course. You naturally look to the point of pain in order to heal the pain. Yet often when there is emotional pain or psychological pain, instead of looking to the heart or to the mind, we go and look at the television or we go to the liquor bottle or to the refrigerator. But of course that's not where the pain is. Then, because we didn't listen to our friend, pain, a pain that could have been remedied, turns into suffering, the suffering of addiction, or of shame or of isolation.

If a hurt child comes to a good parent and says, "Mommy, my heart aches," the good parent doesn't run away from the child, doesn't tell the child, "Go away now and watch a TV show, or go masturbate with some pornography, or go get stoned." The good parent holds the child, calms, soothes, and loves the child, and the child's pain becomes a source of compassion, a lesson in compassion for the child and the parent, a cause of love and healing.

But the bad parent puts the child in front of a TV or gives them a sweet treat, or is too busy or incompetent to bother with their child's pain and turns away or worse, says to them, "I'll give you something real to cry about." So instead of the child's pain being an opportunity for compassion, it becomes the root of suffering, often life-long suffering.

A friend only becomes an enemy when we treat them as one. Pain only becomes suffering when confronted with ignorance.

good fruit

If we are really to "judge a tree by its fruit," we have a big problem. What exactly constitutes good fruit?

Once our tastes are perverted, even rotten fruit may be something we desire. Once our eyes and our minds are closed to what's real, how can we see and know? Even greed, power madness and gluttony may seem delectable to those who are impoverished, powerless or starving, and worst of all, the ignorant may fear the wise.

critics

The only opinions I seek and cherish are from those who really know me. The only way to know anyone is to love them. This of course, makes the field of professional criticism thoroughly suspect, as it should be.

Judgmentalism is the manifestation of an underdeveloped mind seeking security from itself.

Wisdom

The greatest gift is wisdom. The second greatest is a wise friend.

Without wisdom, whatever you have that is good will be squandered, be it health or wealth or friendship or love.

With wisdom, whatever is wrong can be traced back to its cause and healed or corrected.

Wisdom is understanding. Its application is appropriateness.

Wisdom is the point where compassion and knowledge meet and make us whole. But if you lack wisdom, how will you know it? And how will you know if your friend is wise? Because they tell you so?

The test of wisdom is simple: If someone values wisdom above all else, then they are wise.

humility

Perhaps the biggest obstacle to wisdom — which is knowledge of the real — is belief. The dark side of belief is that if I believe in something that isn't true, then it closes my mind and heart to the possibility of finding what is true.

Yet without belief, no progress can be made. If I don't believe in possibility then I won't explore. And if I don't believe there's gold in them thar' hills, then I won't start digging.

Now let's say you've been digging and digging for a long time and you have a deep hole but no gold. You dug in the wrong place and you're disgusted and tired and just feel like you've wasted so much time and effort. Do not despair. Stand in that empty hole and disavow your belief and cry out, "I was wrong! My view was wrong! Please help me!" And in that moment, you may learn where one should *always start* digging.

surrender

Surrender I have found is the right way to live. Why surrender? Because there is no such thing as unaided effort.

waves

Real life is effortless. Really, it is. The situation includes everything, the energy, insight, knowledge and of course, you. When you make an effort, a vibration is set up that stirs up the space between you and the rest of what's happening. That vibration creates a wave of distortion and disruption. Since it is love that connects everything as it already is, and since you cannot improve on love, why make waves?

claiming

So, how do you stop trying? How do you surrender? Well, how do you breathe or digest or grow? I'll tell you, I don't know. You don't know. There you go. We've just surrendered.

"He who claims to know, knows nothing. He who claims nothing, knows."

inadequate

The self I have *become* is inadequate. This is not a judgment, it's a fact. The path I was given by others is inadequate, so now my efforts are inadequate, inadequate to what I wish to give, to share, to offer, inadequate compared to the depth of my feelings. Inadequate to express that truth, that love, that god or goddess of my heart, inadequate to heal that which is broken. Inadequate in so much that really matters.

That is not to say that there is nothing that is adequate. There is, in fact, something that is more than adequate. How can I find this something? This illumination? This excellent, articulate, healing friend of friends? By knowing the self I have been given as inadequate, and caring so much for the self that I have lost, which is the Real, the Virtuous, and the Principled, my mind and heart break with the frustration of my inadequacy and melt with the heat of my passionate search, and release that which is always there in Reality. Through surrender of my inadequacy, I find what's Real.

Socrates said, "The unexamined life is not worth living."

Whatever reason you have for sadness, fear, anger, hatred, greed, lust, or any other "bad" thing, I have complete faith that your reasons are rooted in something that is basically sane and right, rooted in your own goodness. I'm not just saying that and I'm not excusing it.

Every distortion of love is just that- a distortion of *love*. Love is the ground, the thread. Every distortion of reality has reality as its basis. Every distortion of goodness has goodness as its basis, its fundamental material.

The key is to follow the thread and trace the distortion back to its source. Sherlock Holmes and the Ancient Greeks called this process deductive reasoning. You trace an effect back to its cause or its "reason."

You may find that in everything that is bad about your life, there is a common thread of harm or hurt. The important part is to care to understand what really hurt you because in trying to understand, you actually untie the cause of the harm which has always been misunderstanding rooted in insufficient care. Check it out.

meditation

There are two meditations. There is the practice, which is returning the mind again and again to the object of attention, be it the breath or a mantra, prayer or image. This practice is to strengthen the power of the attention and to "correct" the mind's roving and fickle ways. It is something that you can learn. It is a tool.

Then there is the reality of meditating. It is not a practice. It cannot be learned. It does not need to be learned. It is there already and has always been there. It is innate.

The first method requires effort where this is effortless. The other is called spiritual work, and this, the Grace of Spirit. In this meditation, one *rests* in the space between objects and in the "no time" between moments. This meditation is the point where everything meets. It is a full emptiness, complete communication, communion. Here, the mind is joined to the heart, the individual to the Universe. It is where the transitory and the Eternal are one, where Wisdom and ignorance, being and becoming, and all conflicting principles are joined and reconciled. It is where the lowest and the highest have common ground, where desire finds satisfaction and fear is comforted. It is where "the lion lies down with the lamb." It is the actual Love, the most sensitive, the perfectly harmless, the Tao, Nirvana. It is our natural state, our own real mind without all the cultural, religious and scientific bullshit we've been poisoned by.

conflict resignation

What we call conflict is really a misalignment of thought, emotion and action. This is equally true within us and between us. That is because conflict is the disparity between what you know in your heart to be real and what you are forced to believe in order to fit in.

It is what you resign yourself to when you say, "I give up," on those beautiful days when you are locked in a classroom as a child, or when you don't question your local priest or rabbi when they say something irrational, or when you kiss the aunt you don't like, or when you buy what the ads tell you to buy even though you don't need it, and every time you are forced to become someone you are not, like the person who goes to an office every single day until the end.

-ism

Why so much struggle, so much conflict? All the talk of peace and love, all the so-called saints, all the precepts, commandments, instructions and teachings, and we are in a deeper pile of "who-did-it-and-ran" than ever. Why? Because the only good –ism is jism. No kidding. Isms just make schisms.

The Real is waiting with open arms. But who wants to be disillusioned? It's interesting that there's no such word as "dis-realitied."

smile

So are you smiling? Why not? If not, please use the remainder of this page to list your reasons. If extra paper is needed, go get some. If you are smiling, you can go to the next page.

considering consequences

I've never heard anyone say, "Hey honey, let's get married and have an adolescent."

Or…"If I believe that my sins created torment for the best of men I won't feel guilty."

service

I've noticed that when things are bad, when I feel bad, I feel alone and I want to isolate. But when things are good, I feel connected and energized. Why should this be?

I need love, I need connectedness "more" when I'm upset, when I'm lost, when I have problems. Yet that is when I'm most likely to go off somewhere and isolate. And that only makes me feel worse.

I think this misunderstanding has to do with shame, has to do with failure. It has to do with not having someone to turn to when we were little and felt sad and/or only being rewarded when we succeeded. This is why I want to share my successes and I want to hide my failures. I want to share my pleasures and hide my pain. Clearly that is not a recipe for healing. The happy part of me is already A-Okay. But the part of me that wants to hide my pain, not so much. If I go to the doctor and hide my pain, how can he help me? How can someone be a friend to me if I won't even let them in?

Exactly what is it that makes someone unworthy of love? To have failed? We all know that the only person who has never failed is the one who has never tried anything. Yet what could make us feel worse than to turn away from love, or in our hour of need, to refuse a helping hand or a healing heart? And isn't it true that what makes us feel worst of all is when we know we can help someone and they won't let us in.

falling "into" Grace

Close your eyes, open your mind turn your palms to the heavens and just fall into the unknown. That's the best way I have found to face life and to serve my fellow beings.

knowledge

The fool fears the unknown while the wise man delights in the possibilities it affords.

I am inflamed by the passion for learning and my fire extinguished having known. One of the most important signs of life is warmth. Nothing is behind me. Everything lies before me. God, how exciting it is to be a child in a man's body!

~

          I must write a poem or my heart will burst,

          in writing I find that first is last and last is first,

          as the poem itself is the bursting heart

          and I am bleeding the moment I start.

~

This writing is not words or print or thoughts or feelings, it is a frail attempt at communion. To reach you I reach to myself. To reach myself I reach out to you. This writing is a hand holding a heart, holding a life, and the hand is open.

tao

The Real flows! When I find the Real, my hard and fast view of myself and the world dissolves into a flowing thing, a unity, a big, super-intelligent, playful, powerful, caring, perfect "IT."

IT does everything. My efforts only interfere. IT is perfect in its appropriateness for it knows everything from the inside. IT has this amazing harmlessness that leaves everything it touches intact but made new again. IT is joy beyond imagining, understanding beyond imagining and a life that is without reference in time or space, a Now that is happening too fast to be captured, a spontaneous, erupting, flowering continuum that is always just this and just this and just this and just this ...

Reality, what a concept. And IT's *FUN!*

cosmic, dude

Everything is already cosmic consciousness. It simply goes unnoticed. People are pre-occupied with ideas, with beliefs about life that remain unquestioned, even though the life this produces is dissatisfying.

So right now the IT is here, as completely and holy as It was to Moses, a Nirvana as perfect right now as it was to the Buddha, yet people are blind to it. *Life* is never going to be better than it is right now. Life is not the problem. Nothing can make it better, but we don't see it that way. Our view is the problem, not our situation, not the world, our view. Our view is that the world is the problem, so instead of looking at ourselves, we look at the world. Don't work on the world. Work on the view. Uncover the inadequacy of the view and *the wrong view* will fall away and then we will see. To paraphrase a famous Jewish carpenter who is not Norm Abrams, before we take the itty bitty piece of dust out of someone else's eye, we should take the 2x10 out of our own.

monkeys

I've heard intelligent people say that there is no intelligent causal agent to the universe, no God. That if one thousand monkeys were to tap at one thousand typewriters, they would eventually, by sheer happenstance, write *Hamlet*. First of all, why *Hamlet*? Why not *Finnegan's Wake* or the Book of Revelations, which might have seemed at least slightly plausible. But more to the point, I can't help but wonder how did the monkeys get all those typewriters?

Update: A year ago I gave a thousand monkeys typewriters, and as a control group, I gave a thousand humans typewriters. Today, the monkeys presented me with *When Hamlet Met Sally*, *Return to the Planet of the Apes*, *Curious George Discovers America,* and a collaborative research paper on *The Origin of Species*.

The humans gave me *Mein Kampf* and *Horton Hears a Who!* Nice.

bricks

If you were building a house, you could not take the bricks that are in the foundation to build the next level. Yet we continue to try to use the things we were given in the past to build up a life in the here and now. Just as the house would collapse on itself, so the life does as well. We need the new material to build upward and outward. It is no good to cling to and to reuse the old material.

really

When people are unnatural, they see the natural as supernatural. This is the basic misconception of religion. People who are natural are awake. They manifest presence, understanding and joy. This is not a teaching. It is simply the way things are altogether. To make the utterances of a person who is simply natural into a teaching is to entirely miss the point.

There is no supernatural being. There is something much greater. There is that which is Real and natural. It is beyond the grasp, beyond the harm of the unnatural and the unreal. There is no achieving what is and what has always been there. Let go of the wrong view. Let go of the supernatural. Let go of all these things that seem distant and you can find exactly what other people have found: the natural way that is forever and ever right here and now.

equality

Equality is spirit. Spirit cannot be modified, cannot be larger or smaller, better or worse, richer or poorer, and in this way, what is Real in us is equal to what is real in everyone. That is why I say that the whole concept of saints and buddhas and avatars is simply an ego trick, a virtual reality that when seen correctly, vanishes.

Life is not an athletic competition or a qualifying exam. Bodies and brains are different, some stronger, some not, more or less agile or proficient. Not so with Spirit. Beyond appearance is the Real, and the Real is equal to Itself everywhere.

behind the curtain

As a child I had the conviction that there was a curtain in front of me at all times and if I could just grab the edge and pull it aside, an entirely different and far more substantial and beautiful world would be revealed. It turned out I was right.

When the curtain parted, this world of appearances was seen as an illusion and the sub-stratum seen as a timeless, formless, being-ness, free of suffering, turmoil, conflict and foolishness and possessed of boundless joy and understanding.

I promise you, this is not a pipe dream or wishful thinking. It is a direct perception of Reality and has been reported time and again, in all corners of the world, throughout history by people from all walks of life.

friendship

What I would like is to always seek and share the Good and True. Friendship is the best thing ever. Since the Good has no end, seeking and sharing would have no end. So our friendship would be forever.

baseball

"You just have to see the ball. Just follow the ball. Your bat, your glove, will naturally do the right thing."

Seeing is not doing. It is receiving. It is openness. Straining to see distorts the view. What might have appeared beautiful undistorted now may be ugly and frightening. In a funhouse mirror, even Miss America is homely.

Yogi-ism

What people really need are four or five good habits that they do non-habitually.

pathos

It is said that we fear the unknown. But how can we have fear of something that has not yet happened? We can only say, "I don't know." Really we fear what we know, based only on our misconception of what has already happened, and project that into what has not happened yet. This actually turns infinite possibility into a finite misery. There is a sad comfort in limitation. The Greeks called it *pathos*.

home

Who doesn't want to feel secure? Who doesn't want to feel safe?

But what is safety? Security? Everything is, in reality, impermanent except reality. It's always changing *yet It* is always the same. Picture a tire rolling along the road. Every second a new point of contact. The road winding on. The tire wearing down, always different. Never the same tire exactly, never the same spot of road. But where they meet is *always where they meet. Where everything meets is always new but always the same.* Where everything meets is what people call God or love. That's the Real. Always brand new and fresh, always the same, like coming home. The same but different. Just like all of us.

Heraclitus said, "We never step in the same river twice." *That's true but yes we do, too.*

education

Learning is a great joy, isn't it? Discovery's a great joy. It's like being a little kid again and again. It's like the first morning.

I think one common human denominator is the love of learning. And of course we have to love, at least a little, to really learn, or to learn by heart, because our heart has to be in it, not just our head or some other body part.

So what do we need in order to learn? A subject of study. Well, that's a funny thing since we are always the subject no matter what's being studied. Anything outside of us would be an object of our study in which we would remain the subject. So without a single object we already have the subject of learning, which is us.

Do we also need curiosity or wonder, an open curious mind and attitude? If I already know, or believe I know, or am not interested for any reason in my subject, which is myself, my mind will certainly not be into it, much less my heart. So for my heart to be into learning, I need to love what I'm studying. I need to love the subject, which is me. If I were a teacher and I didn't love the student, then how would I treat that student? Will my heart go out to that student? Will I wish to give them what is most wonderful and interesting? Will I really know what's best for the student without caring about them? Could I possibly be enthusiastic or encouraging 'without love?

Now, if I really love the subject, which is myself, will I not know in my heart what is best or not best, as I feel the need as my own? And then am I not a fitting guide or teacher or friend to myself? So to love the subject of learning which is myself, , is the root of proper learning, which is perhaps the greatest gift of being human. What a nice, practical arrangement.

So at Delphi, when those old timers inscribed, "Know Thyself," they were telling us the basis of all Real education.

and the pursuit of happiness

The reason why looking for a result usually makes us driven and sad instead of happy is that we already have and are what we have been looking for.

death

Life after death? Reincarnation? Where are the postcards? The letters? "You've been dead over a year already and not one phone call!"

One thing is clear. It is everyone's experience that absolutely nothing whatsoever is permanent. So why should death be?

passing

Dead friends where are you now,

lovely girls and fine young men,

pictured as I saw you last I do my best to hold you fast,

So afraid that you may at any moment slip away,

to the shore,

across the sea,

from the tear in my heart,

called memory.

navigating authority

A sailor knows that in order to find his position, he needs more than one "fix" or point of reference. In other words, to know where he is in the middle of the ocean, he has to triangulate coordinates based on his relationship to more than one fixed or known object.

We should never base our view of ourselves, which of course is our position in life, on just one fix from one relationship no matter how significant.

not your boat

A good friend who is rich and has a nice boat is much better than owning your own boat. I've owned seventeen boats, but my friend Chucky's boat was always more fun that any of the boats I had. You don't have to own something to enjoy it.

Love is like that. Most people want to be loved so much that it becomes a desperation which is not loving at all. So two people desperate for love meet and then they "fall" in what exactly? Love? How? Neither one is bringing love, just desperation.

Love is not something to possess. It's something to pass on or more accurately to acknowledge joyously as what is already there. Why don't we see that love is already there? Deep down we know it is. We see it sometimes and other times we feel ourselves resist seeing it. Sometimes at a concert when everyone is singing, or after a really fine film, or at an art exhibit, or when standing before a wonder of nature, we feel the connectedness in our appreciation and our sharing. Sharing the moment, sharing life, sharing this amazing gift. We are all sharing this amazing gift of life all the time. So you see, it is already there. Love, I mean. So we all share this amazing gift all the time. And that's love. That's reality. So desperation comes from not seeing that. Unhappiness comes from not seeing that. Loneliness comes from not seeing that.

Your Friend is really rich and He's really your Friend and He wants company, your company on His boat. Just someone there, with Him, to appreciate the sea, and the sky, and His good fortune. Isn't that nice?

potatoes

People often talk about their personal reality but I believe that we share a common reality. I don't deny that there are many viewpoints, but those viewpoints are of one thing. Conflict arises not only because of the differing viewpoints but because we are all affected by each other's sharing that one reality.

I've heard that a long time ago when sailors wanted to clean potatoes, they would take a bunch of potatoes and put them in a bucket filled with water. Then they would let the motion of the ship going back and forth scrub those potatoes clean. As human beings, we're going to have to be patient because we're dealing with a very big bucket and a shitload of potatoes.

Dust

Dust upon the sill am I
        I am the stuff of earth and sky
Floating in a shaft of light
        Stardust drifting through the night

In the dark dream I am falling
        In the daybreak I am calling

        Remember me
        Remember me
     Drifting, falling, floating
        FREE

        (2013)

In Japanese "kokoro" means "heart," the deepest, best place of a human being.

Kokoro Press titles are written from that place, to that place in you. Our heart to your heart.

www.kokoropress.com